All Things CAPYBARAS For Kids

FILLED WITH PLENTY OF FACTS, PHOTOS, AND FUN TO LEARN ALL ABOUT CAPYBARAS

ANIMAL READS

WWW.ANIMALREADS.COM

THIS BOOK BELONGS TO...

_____

_____

WWW.ANIMALREADS.COM

BENEATH THE BIG FLUFF:
WHAT'S INSIDE?

Welcome to the World of Capybaras! 1

What Even Is This Animal?! 5

Capybara Body 13
   Basics & Personality

Capybaras & Water— 25
   The Perfect Match

Where in the World 33
   Are the Capybaras?

What's on the Capybara Menu? 41

Meet the Capybara Family 51

Growing Up the Capybara Way 57

Weird, Wonderful, and Totally Capybara 67

You're Now a Certified Capy Captain! 73

Thank You! 77

WELCOME TO THE WORLD OF CAPYBARAS!

Have you ever seen an animal that looks like a giant guinea pig with a secret swimming talent? Or maybe you've spotted something that looks like a dark brown potato with legs relaxing by a pond?

Meet the capybara—nature's champion of chilling out and making friends.

"So what makes capybaras so special?" you might ask. Well, imagine your pet guinea pig suddenly grew to the size of a medium dog, developed webbed toes like tiny flippers, and could hold its breath underwater for five minutes! Pretty impressive, right? Well, that's what makes a capybara … a capybara!

In this book, we'll dive into the world of these gentle giants. You'll discover how their bodies are built for swimming and snacking. You'll also learn why they're so good at making friends and what helps them stay safe in the wild. Every part of a capybara has something interesting to share, from their sharp teeth to their waterproof fur.

So grab your imaginary swim goggles and get ready to explore. By the end of this book, you'll be a certified capybara expert—ready to wow your friends and family with some truly wild facts.

Let's dive in!

WHAT EVEN IS THIS ANIMAL?!

Capybaras are one of those animals that make you do a double take. They look a bit like giant guinea pigs—and that's not far off! In fact, capybaras are the **biggest rodents** in the world.

They can grow as long as a golden retriever and weigh up to **150 pounds** (68 kilograms)—that's heavier than many fourth graders!

Fun Fact:

*The name "capybara" comes from a South American language called **Tupi**. In Tupi, they were called kapiyva, which means **"master of the grasses."** A perfect name for an animal that spends most of its day munching on green plants!*

But capybaras aren't just big—they're also incredibly friendly. They're known for being social, relaxed, and peaceful. They live in groups, get along with other animals like birds, monkeys, and even

crocodiles, and always find a way to share space. It's no wonder they've become favorites among humans and animals.

FUZZY, FRIENDLY, AND FULL OF SURPRISES

Capybaras are **mammals**—just like us, our pets, and many zoo animals. That means they have fur, are warm-blooded, and the mothers feed their babies milk.

Capybaras have short, coarse fur that helps them dry off quickly after a swim. Their babies, called **pups**, are born fully furred, with open eyes, and ready to explore. And like all mammals, they're warm-blooded, which helps them stay active whether the day is hot or cool.

Instead of laying eggs like reptiles or birds, **mammal** mothers give birth to live babies, and capy**baras** are no exception. From day one, a baby capybara is part of the group, learning to graze, swim, and stay safe.

RODENT ROYALTY

Scientists sort animals into groups to help us understand how they're related—kind of like sorting books on a shelf or toys into bins. Along with being mammals, capybaras also belong to the **rodent** group, just like mice, rats, squirrels, beavers, porcupines, and guinea pigs.

A rodent is an animal with **big front teeth that never stop growing**—perfect for nibbling and gnawing. To keep their teeth from getting too long, rodents chew on hard things like plants, wood, or bark. This also keeps their teeth nice and sharp!

Fun Fact:

*Did you know that **about 40% of all mammals** are rodents? That means almost half the world's mammals share the same kind of teeth!*

With teeth that never stop growing, I've got to keep chewing!

Capybaras are part of a rodent family called **Caviidae**, which includes guinea pigs and rock cavies. So yes—they really are cousins to guinea pigs, not just lookalikes!

Their scientific name is *Hydrochoerus hydrochaeris*. It sounds tricky, but it actually means **"water pig"**—a perfect fit for this water-loving rodent.

BORN FOR THE GOOD LIFE

Many rodents like to dig or scurry around, but capybaras have a different kind of lifestyle. They're **semi-aquatic**—"semi" means "partly," and "aquatic" means "water," so "semi-aquatic" means an animal that lives partly in water and partly on land.

While most rodents actively avoid water, capybaras thrive in it. They're excellent swimmers, thanks to their **webbed feet**, which act like paddles. They can glide through rivers, float in shallow pools, and even sleep with just their noses poking out above the surface.

And unlike many small animals that prefer to hide, capybaras are calm and confident. You'll often see them relaxing out in the open, sitting beside a riverbank, or wandering through tall grass with their group.

So, what *is* a capybara? It's not just the world's largest rodent. It's one of the friendliest, most chilled-out animals on the planet—built for life in water, made to munch on grass, and perfectly designed to stay calm in the wild.

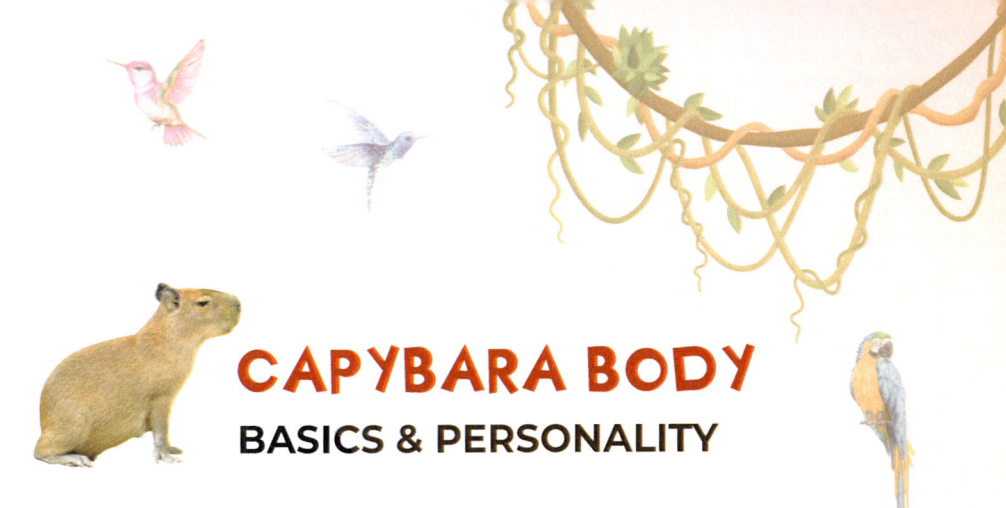

CAPYBARA BODY
BASICS & PERSONALITY

I f you had to invent the perfect animal for life on both land and in water, you'd end up with something a lot like a capybara. From head to toe, their bodies are built to swim, stay comfortable in any weather, and move easily through muddy wetlands.

Let's take a closer look at all the features that make capybaras perfectly suited for their one-of-a-kind way of life.

A BODY BUILT TO FLOAT

Capybaras have a **barrel-shaped body** that's wide, round, and perfect for floating. This shape spreads their weight evenly and helps them stay **buoyant** in the water, *meaning they can float without too much effort.* Their quirky body shape also helps them manage body temperature. They can cool off quickly on hot days and stay warm on cooler ones, as if they have a built-in thermostat!

Fun Fact:

Adult capybaras are about **3.5 to 4.5 feet (107 to 137 cm)** long—roughly the length of an adult bicycle—and **1.5 to 2 feet (46 to 61 cm)** tall at the shoulder. That's about as tall as a kitchen table! They can weigh anywhere from **77 to 150 pounds (35 to 68 kg)**, about the same as a large dog.

FLIPPERS, TOES, AND SNOUTY SUPERPOWERS

One of the first things you'll notice about capybaras is that their **eyes, ears, and noses sit high on their heads.** Thanks to this clever placement, they can stay underwater but still breathe, see, and hear what's happening. Nature gave them the perfect design for sneaky swimming—they can see what's happening above water while keeping most of their body safely below!

Their feet are also perfectly shaped for swimming. Capybaras have slightly webbed toes, with

These feet were made for walking... and swimming too!

skin between them that acts like mini-flippers. These webbed feet let them paddle smoothly through rivers, lakes, and muddy ground.

Their front feet have four toes, and their back feet have three. This gives them just the right combination for moving through wet, squishy places.

Even their toes are totally unique. Instead of sharp claws like other animals, capybaras have more rounded nails, which help them walk easily on land and in water.

> My head and fur are perfect for swimming! My nose, eyes, and ears all sit up high—just the way a swimmer needs them!

ROUGH, TOUGH, AND WATERPROOF

A capybara's fur is **coarse and waterproof,** so it dries quickly after a swim. Their coloring—usually reddish-brown, dark brown, or even gray—helps them blend into muddy riverbanks and grassy fields. This makes it easier for them to stay hidden from predators while relaxing near the water's edge.

Fun Fact:

*Here's something unexpected ... **capybaras don't have tails!** Just a small bump where a tail would be. Since they don't need one for balance or climbing like squirrels, nature decided they could do without it!*

Who needs a tail when you've got a fluffy caboose like this?

I'm not yelling—I'm chewing dramatically!

CHOMPING CHAMPS

If you could peek inside a capybara's mouth, you'd notice something unusual: the front of their teeth is **bright orange**. That's because their tooth enamel contains **iron**, which makes them stronger and harder than regular teeth—perfect for life as a full-time plant muncher!

Capybaras also chew in a unique way. While we move our jaws up and down, capybaras move theirs **side to side**, as camels do. This grinding motion

helps them break thick grasses into smaller, easier-to-digest pieces. But eating isn't the only thing they're built for—capybaras also have excellent **senses** to help them stay safe.

THE CAPYBARA'S SUPER SENSES

A capybara's **hearing** is especially sharp. Even though their ears are small and round, they can swivel in different directions to catch sounds from all around—helpful when they're quietly grazing near a river.

I may look relaxed, but I'm tuned in to every sound and smell!

Their **sense of smell** is just as powerful. A moist nose helps them pick up scents in the air, telling them what's nearby—whether it's fresh grass or a potential predator.

And, while their **eyesight** may not be their strongest sense, their wide-set eyes give them a broad view of the world. This makes it easier to spot danger coming from almost any direction.

GENTLE SOULS IN FURRY COATS

One of the most special things about capybaras is how **friendly** they are. We know we've said it before, but it's worth repeating!

These gentle animals live in groups called **herds**, which can include 10 to 40 members or more. They spend their days relaxing, grazing, grooming each other, and keeping an eye out for danger. If one

capybara senses something a little off, it may bark to warn the others, and the whole group will react.

Capybaras don't fight much. Instead, they rely on touch, soft sounds, and body language to get along. *It's a peaceful way to live, don't you think?*

But what really sets them apart is how well they get along with other animals, not just their own kind. Birds often ride on their backs. Monkeys play nearby. Even caiman (*relatives of crocodiles*) sometimes share the same riverside without any trouble.

Scientists don't fully understand why capybaras are so good at making friends, but it probably comes from their calm, gentle nature. They're not aggressive or bossy—they just go with the flow.

Capybaras also have their own way of **talking**. They use a mix of sounds—like **whistles**, **clicks**,

We're so friendly, even our predators enjoy chilling with us.

barks, and **purrs**—to communicate their feelings or to send a message. They also use **body language** to share information, like ear movements or sitting in a group.

Now that we know how their bodies are tailor-made for water, let's see how capybaras actually live their day-to-day lives in the water!

Peaceful, patient, and always side by side.

ALL FUR ONE,

AND ONE FUR ALL!

CAPYBARAS & WATER—
THE PERFECT MATCH

I f capybaras could join the Animal Olympics, they'd be strong contenders for gold in swimming, relaxing, and water-based napping!

Thanks to their floating shape, webbed feet, and waterproof coats, capybaras don't just dip into water—they *live* in it.

Let's dive into what makes capybaras some of nature's most fascinating aquatic experts.

BORN TO PADDLE

Capybaras are what scientists call **semi-aquatic** animals—they live partly on land and partly in water. While some animals avoid getting wet, capybaras feel right at home in rivers, lakes, and marshes. They can even **hold their breath for up to five minutes!**

Even baby capybaras can swim shortly after birth. While human babies need lessons, capybara pups

instinctively know how to paddle and float. It's almost like swimming is part of their DNA.

BELOW THE SURFACE

Capybaras are full of surprises underwater, too. They can **close their ears and nostrils** when they dive to keep water out—ideal for escaping danger or searching for food below the surface.

One of their most surprising skills? **Sleeping while floating.** That's right—capybaras can take naps in shallow water, with just their nose sticking out to breathe. Nature basically gave them their own floating mattress!

They can also **walk along the bottoms of shallow ponds or streams,** using their weight to stay grounded as they look for tasty plants.

WHY CAPYBARAS NEVER STRAY FAR FROM WATER

Water isn't just fun for capybaras—it's essential.

- It helps them **cool down**. Capybaras live in warm parts of South America. Since they don't sweat like humans, swimming helps them stay comfortable in the heat.
- It offers **protection**. If a predator gets too close, a capybara can dive and disappear, using the water as a safe escape route.
- It's where they find **food**. Many of their favorite plants grow in or near water, and being great swimmers means they can reach snacks others can't.
- And yes—it's just **plain fun**. Young capybaras splash and play while adults float peacefully during the hottest parts of the day.

No stress. No rush. Just floating along!

WORLD CLASS SWIMMERS

Some animals are famous swimmers—like beavers with paddle tails or otters with sleek bodies—but capybaras have their own special way of swimming that works perfectly for their lifestyle.

Scientists have even seen them **cross wide rivers** and **swim through strong currents.** When floods happen, they swim long distances to find dry land and new places to eat.

Whether they're cooling off, escaping danger, searching for snacks, or just floating with friends,

capybaras are true swimming champions. They've turned the rivers and wetlands of South America into their own calm, watery playground.

So next time you're enjoying a swim or a warm bath, think of your capybara friends—doing the same thing somewhere in the wild, with their noses above water and their group nearby.

Who knew the world's biggest rodent could also be one of its best swimmers?

WHEN CAPYBARAS THROW A PARTY, YOU KNOW IT'S GOING TO BE A SPLASH!

WHERE IN THE WORLD
ARE THE CAPYBARAS?

If you wanted to visit a capybara in its natural home, you'd need to head to **South America**. These relaxed, water-loving animals have made their homes in some of the continent's most beautiful wetlands, rivers, and grassy forests.

Let's explore where capybaras live—and what makes these places such a perfect fit.

DESIGNING THE PERFECT CAPY PARADISE

Capybaras are pretty particular when it comes to picking the right home. They need three key things to be happy:

1. **Water** for swimming and staying cool
2. **Grass and plants** for grazing
3. **Trees or bushes** for shade and shelter

They're most often found in **wetlands**—areas where the land is partly covered in shallow water during parts of the year. These include **marshes**, **swamps**, and the grassy edges of rivers and lakes.

Capybaras can splash, graze, nap, and keep an eye out for danger in these places. They move calmly through the landscape, and as they do, they actually help shape it. Over time, their footsteps create narrow trails through the grass, like tiny capybara highways connecting their favorite spots.

They're also tidier than you might expect. Groups of capybaras often use the same areas as **bathroom spots**, a bit away from where they eat and rest. Scientists believe this helps keep their living areas clean and may reduce the spread of parasites or diseases. Smart *and* sanitary!

CAPYBARAS ON THE MAP

Capybaras live across much of **central and eastern South America.** They prefer places with warm temperatures and year-round water.

Here are some of their favorite regions:

- **Brazil**—Home to the **Pantanal**, the world's largest wetland, Brazil has more capybaras than anywhere else. It's like a capybara paradise, filled with rivers, ponds, and endless grass.
- **Venezuela**—The **llanos**, or grassy plains, flood seasonally, creating an ideal habitat for capybaras.

Here's a simple look at where capybaras live in South America! It's not a perfect map, but it shows their favorite spots.

- **Colombia**—River systems and wetlands here support large populations of capybaras.
- **Argentina**—Especially in the north, around rivers and marshes, capybaras thrive.
- **Peru, Ecuador, Bolivia, Paraguay, and Uruguay**—Wetlands and river areas in these countries are also home to capybara groups.

Many capybaras live in or near the **Amazon River basin**, a massive area with countless streams, flooded forests, and grassy banks—just the way they like it.

EVERYBODY LOVES CAPYBARAS

While capybaras are native to South America, their calm personalities have won fans around the world.

In **Japan**, some zoos have even built warm hot spring baths just for capybaras to enjoy during the winter. Photos of them soaking with oranges floating around have become internet favorites!

Some people in other countries have tried keeping capybaras as **exotic pets**, though it's not easy. Capybaras need plenty of space, water access, grass, and constant care. They're not suited to indoor living, and they definitely don't fit in a small backyard.

Capybaras are drawn to water, plants, and peace wherever they go. They always seem to find their place, be it in a South American river or a Japanese hot spring.

WHAT DO CAPYBARAS DO ON WEEKENDS?

Whatever floats their boat!

WHAT'S ON THE CAPYBARA MENU?

If a capybara came over for dinner, you wouldn't need to prepare anything fancy. These gentle giants are strict vegetarians or **herbivores**, meaning they only eat plants. No meat, fish, or insects—just green, leafy goodness from nature's salad bar.

THE DAILY BUFFET

Capybaras spend much of their day eating. Their favorite food? **Grass… and lots of it!**

An adult capybara can eat up to **6–8 pounds (2.7–3.6 kg)** of grass every day. That's roughly the same weight as a bowling ball—or about 25 hamburgers stacked high!

But grass isn't the only thing on the menu. Capybaras enjoy:

1. **Water plants** like reeds and hyacinths are perfect for snacking while they paddle.
2. **Fruits**, especially soft ones that have fallen from trees nearby.

3. **Tree bark**, which may not sound tasty to us but helps wear down the capybara's amazing teeth.

4. **Shrubs and reeds**, especially in dry seasons when grass is harder to find.

Their favorite time to graze is in the early morning or late afternoon when the weather is cooler, and the grass is fresh with dew.

MEALTIME MANNERS

Capybaras are **slow, careful eaters**. They gently nibble their way through grassy areas, always selecting the tastiest plants first. And like everything else they do, capybaras **eat as a team**. While some

We're all about gooood nutrition!

graze, others keep watch for danger, and then they swap roles. It's a quiet, cooperative system that helps the whole herd stay safe and well-fed!

A BRILLIANT DIGESTIVE SYSTEM

Now here's something surprising—but totally normal in the capybara world: *they eat a special kind of their own poop.*

Yep, you read that right.

This behavior is called **coprophagy**, and it's actually a smart way to **recycle nutrients.** The first time food passes through their body, it doesn't get fully digested. So capybaras eat their early-morning

We snack together, we stay safe together.

droppings to give that plant material another round through their digestive system, pulling out even more nutrients the second time.

Other plant-loving animals like **rabbits and guinea pigs** do this too. It may sound gross to us, but in nature, it's genius.

Munching all day might sound relaxing, but in the wild, capybaras know to keep one eye on the grass... and the other on the lookout!

HOW CAPYBARAS STAY SAFE IN THE WILD

Even though capybaras are large, peaceful animals, they're not at the top of the food chain. In the wild, plenty of predators would happily make a meal out of a capybara, especially one that's not paying attention.

That's why these gentle grazers need to always be on the lookout for danger.

WHO'S ON THE HUNT?

Here are some of the predators capybaras need to watch out for:

- **Jaguars**—Powerful big cats that can silently stalk and catch full-grown capybaras.

Capybaras and caimans often chill together—but a young capy has to stay alert!

- **Pumas**—Also known as mountain lions, they may sneak up while capybaras are far from the water.
- **Ocelots**—Smaller wild cats that usually target baby or young capybaras.
- **Anacondas**—Huge snakes that live near water and sometimes grab capybaras when they come close to drink or swim.

- **Caimans**—Relatives of alligators and crocodiles; they wait quietly and may snap at capybaras near the water's edge.
- **Eagles and other large birds of prey**—These can swoop down to carry off capybara pups.

As you see, it's a long list, which is why capybaras are always on alert, even while snacking.

SMART STRATEGIES FOR SAFETY

Capybaras rarely feed alone. They usually graze in **groups**, where some members eat while others

Unusual friends can turn out to be the best of friends!

stand guard. If one senses danger, it lets out a **sharp bark** to warn the rest. Within seconds, the entire group is ready to run—or dive.

Water is their best escape. As soon as something seems wrong, capybaras race into nearby rivers or ponds so they can swim away or dive below the surface and stay hidden for several minutes.

That's why they **always live near water**—it's not just for fun. It's their emergency exit.

BIRDS THAT HELP OUT

Capybaras seem to have a special relationship with a bird called the **caracara** in a few special places.

Help me, help you, help us!

These bold birds often perch on the backs of capybaras or in nearby trees. When a predator is near, the birds call out loudly, giving the capybaras an extra warning.

In return, the caracaras sometimes pick insects from the capybaras' fur or search for bugs stirred up as the herd moves around. Scientists call this a **symbiotic relationship**, where both animals benefit from spending time together.

Even when they look calm and relaxed, capybaras always listen, watch, and stay ready to move. In the wild, being a vegetarian means you've got to stay one step ahead of the meat-eaters.

This little bird is a kiskadee—helpful, chatty, and always welcome on Team Capybara!

CAPYBARA? MORE LIKE HAPPY-BARA!

MEET THE CAPYBARA FAMILY

Did you know there's more than one kind of capybara? While most people picture just one type, scientists have discovered two different species. They may look very similar, but each has its own size, shape, and home range.

Let's take a look at the two official members of the capybara family.

THE COMMON CAPYBARA: BIG, BOLD, AND WELL-KNOWN

When most people think of a capybara, they imagine the **Common Capybara**, also known as the **Larger Capybara**. These are the stars of wildlife documentaries, internet memes, and zoo exhibits around the world.

Their scientific name is *Hydrochoerus hydrochaeris*. This impossible-to-remember name comes from Greek words meaning **"water pig."** Now isn't that a perfect fit for these semi-aquatic giants?!

Common capybaras truly deserve their title as the world's **largest rodents**. Measuring between **3.5 to 4.5 feet (1.1 to 1.4 meters)** from nose to rump—about the length of an adult bicycle—these impressive animals stand **1.5 to 2 feet (45 to 60 cm)** tall. That's roughly the height of a small dog! When fully grown, they can weigh anywhere from **77 to 150 pounds (35 to 70 kg)**—that's like carrying 10-20 bowling balls around!

These water-loving giants live across much of **South America**, especially **Brazil, Venezuela, Colombia, Argentina,** and **Peru.** They're especially common in wet, grassy areas near rivers and marshes, like the massive **Pantanal** wetland and the **Amazon River basin.**

Common capybaras are known to make themselves at home *wherever they go*. Whether lounging in flooded forests or grazing on open plains, they're happy as long as they have water, grass, and plenty of shade.

THE LESSER CAPYBARA: SMALLER BUT JUST AS SPECIAL

Meet the **Lesser Capybara**, sometimes called the **Panama Capybara**. These smaller, more secretive cousins go by the scientific name *Hydrochoerus isthmius*.

I'm a Panama capybara—smaller size, same chill vibes.

They're similar to the Common Capybara but **slightly smaller**. Most measure about **3 to 4 feet (0.9 to 1.2 meters)** long and stand **1 to 1.5 feet (35 to 45 cm)** tall at the shoulder. They weigh less, too, which makes them a bit more agile.

You can sometimes tell them apart by their **narrower face** and slightly different fur color. However, both types are usually some shade of brown or reddish-brown.

These capybaras are found in a much smaller area of Latin America, mainly in **Panama**, **Colombia**, and parts of **Venezuela**. They're often harder to spot because they live in dense forests and along steep riverbanks. Their smaller size helps them climb and move through thick vegetation more easily.

Even with these differences, Lesser Capybaras live a life that's very similar to their larger cousins. They love water, live in groups, eat grasses and aquatic plants, and spend a lot of their time swimming and relaxing near rivers and ponds.

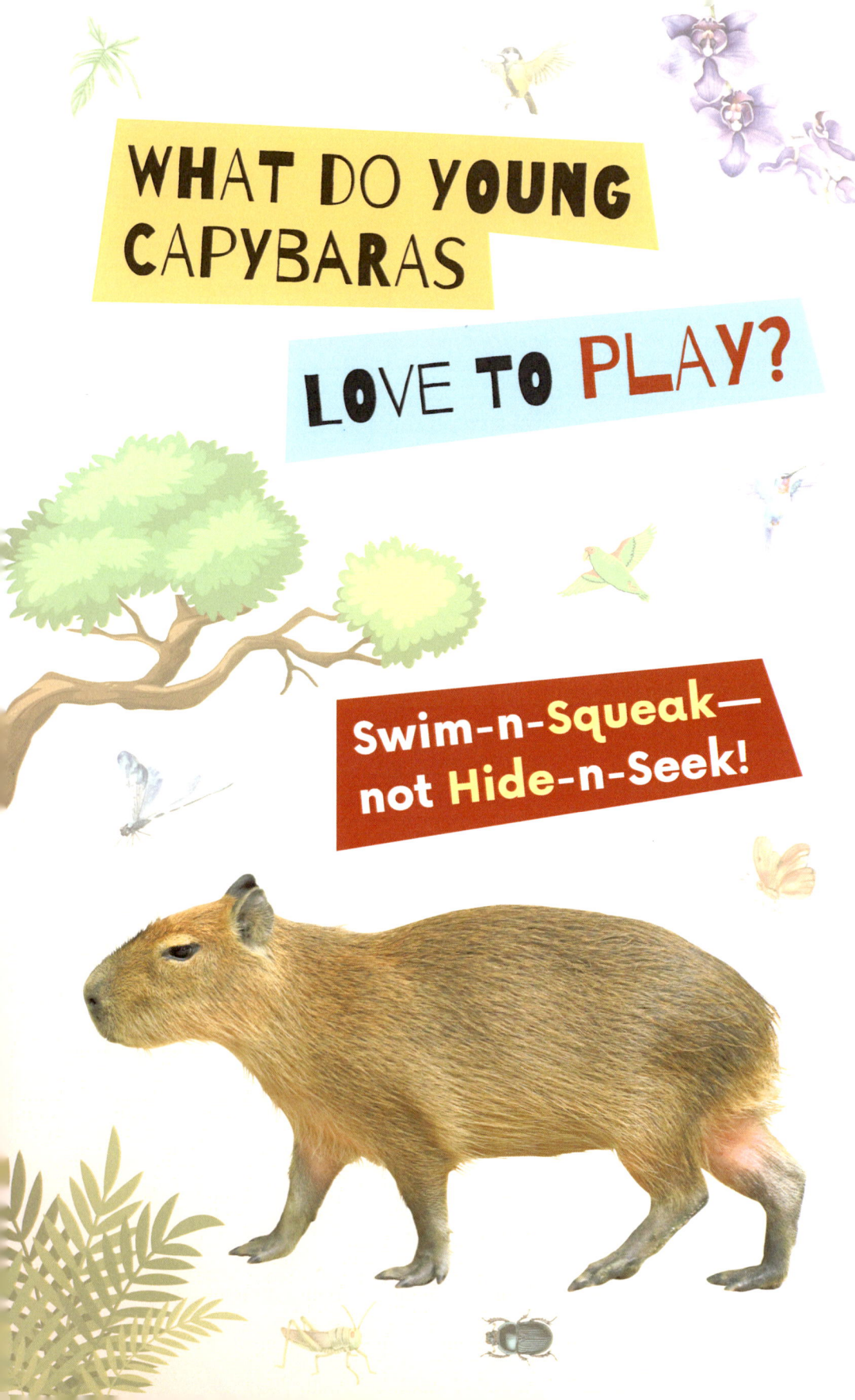

GROWING UP THE CAPYBARA WAY

Every capybara has a big journey—from a tiny pup to a full-grown adult. Like kids, they go through important stages as they grow, learning everything they need to thrive in the wild.

BABY STEPS (0–5 MONTHS)

Capybara pups are born ready for life. They arrive fully furred, eyes open, and can walk, swim, and keep up with the herd within hours. Most mothers have **4 to 8 babies**, after a long pregnancy that lasts around **150 days.**

Newborns weigh around **2–3 pounds (0.9–1.4 kg)** and start drinking their mother's milk immediately. But even in their first week, they begin nibbling grass and copying the adults. They learn super fast—by watching, tasting, and trying everything for themselves.

Baby capybaras often stick together in **nursery groups**, playing, exploring, and swimming with

No crawling stage here—capybara pups are on their feet and moving right away!

other young herd members. The herd shares the work of keeping pups safe, and mothers even take turns babysitting. It's a true group effort!

These early months in a capy's life are all about learning how to spot danger, follow the group, and find the right plants to eat. And it all happens with the help of their family.

CAPY-TEENS (5 MONTHS–1 YEAR)

By five months old, young capybaras stop nursing and eat only plants like adults. This is when

they start looking and acting more like grown-ups, but they're still learning and practicing all the time.

They keep improving in all aspects of capy life: swimming longer, diving deeper, and responding to herd calls. Play still plays a big role in everyday life, as wrestling, chasing, and gentle head-butting help build strength, coordination, and social smarts.

Capybaras also grow quickly at this stage. By their **first birthday**, a young capybara can weigh over **75 pounds (34 kg)** and reach about **75% of adult size**. They're not quite fully mature—but they're well on their way!

> Play wrestling teaches us a lot!

GROWN-UP CAPYBARAS (1+ YEARS)

By the time capybaras are around **1.5 to 2 years old**, they're considered fully grown. Adult females can now have babies, and males might start competing for leadership in the herd.

Capybaras usually live in **groups of 10 to 40 members.** Still, when water becomes scarce during the dry season, even bigger herds may gather around

the last remaining pools. These social groups include adults and youngsters of all ages, led by a **dominant male** who keeps things organized and running smoothly.

LIFE IN THE HERD

Daily life follows a pretty steady rhythm. Capybaras graze in the open in the early morning and late afternoon, then rest in the shade or swim during the heat of the day. At night, when it's cooler, they may head out for more feeding.

Females can have babies twice a year in warm regions. They might raise up to 16 pups every year, though not all will survive. Predators are always nearby, but the herd's teamwork gives the babies a better shot at growing up safely.

In the wild, capybaras live around **8 to 10 years**. Some may reach **12 or even 15 years old** in zoos or protected areas.

WISDOM WITH AGE

Older capybaras might not be the fastest or the loudest, but they've got something even better—

Surprise! It's me—your favorite capy!

wisdom. These calm old-timers often become the quiet leaders of the group. They keep a watchful eye on things, teach the youngsters how to stay out of trouble, and lead by example with their cool, collected style. When one of them sounds the alarm, the whole herd takes notice.

From their wobbly first swims to their wise old soaks, capybaras stick to what they know best: **staying chill, looking out for each other, and living the peaceful life.** In a world full of surprises, these gentle giants prove that **kindness, calm, and community** might just be the best survival tools of all.

WHAT DOES A CAPYBARA WEAR ON ITS HEAD?

A CAP!

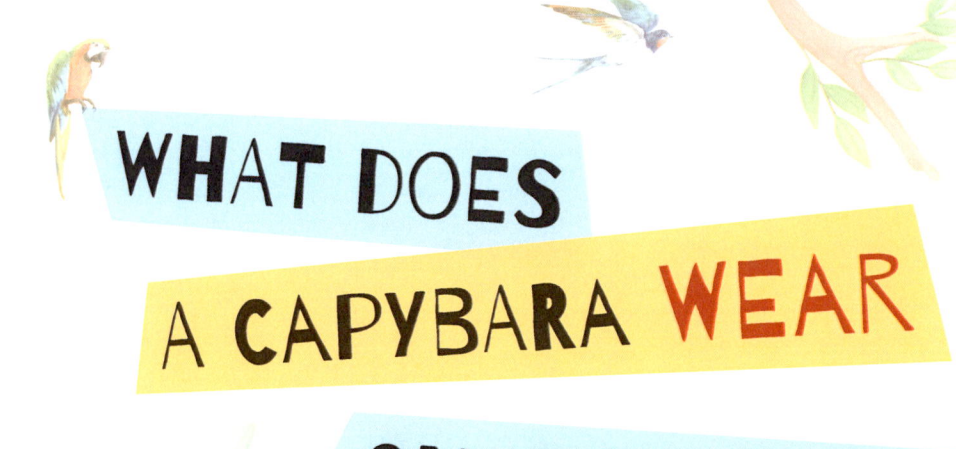

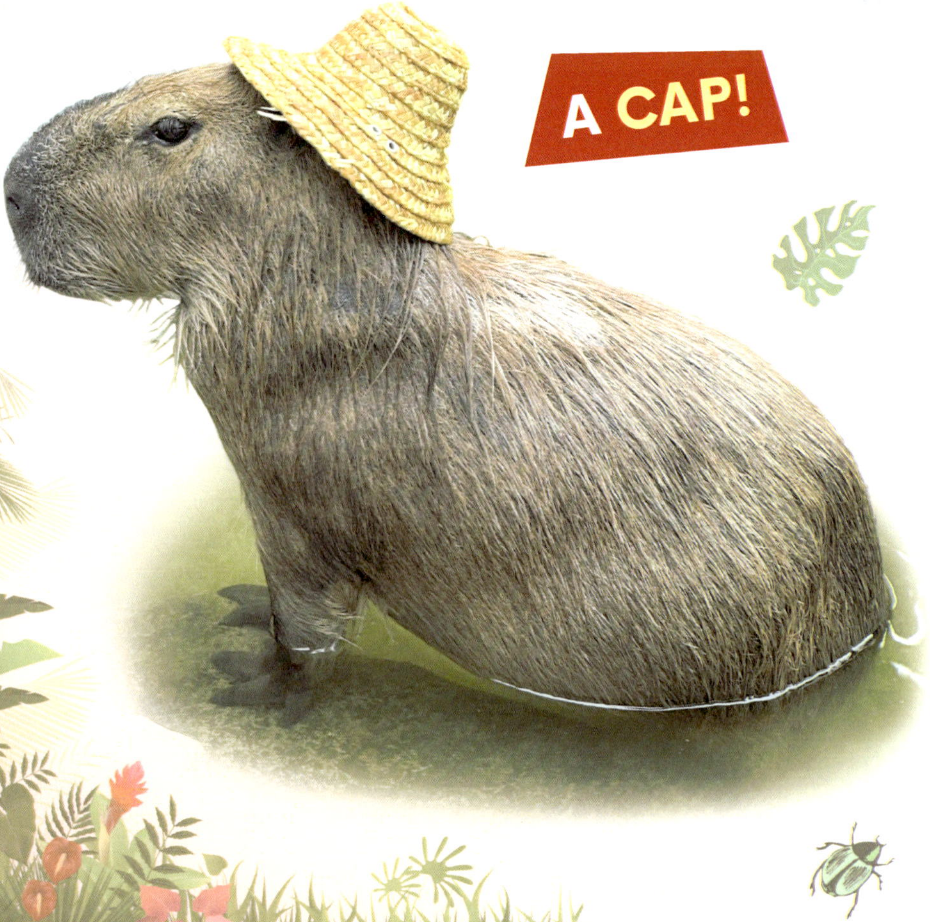

WEIRD, WONDERFUL, AND TOTALLY CAPYBARA

Get ready for the wildest capybara facts of all—these are the kind of fun, surprising, "no way!" discoveries that make capybaras one of the coolest animals on the planet.

Let's dive in!

BUILT-IN SUNSCREEN

Capybaras don't need lotion—they make their own! Their skin secretes a special reddish oil that helps **waterproof their fur** and **protect them from sunburn.** So, if you ever spot a capybara looking a little pinkish? Don't worry—they're not blushing. That's just their **built-in sunscreen doing its job!**

SILENT SWIMMERS AND UNDERWATER SLEEPERS

Capybaras are so relaxed that they can **float and nap in the water**, with just their noses poking out

to breathe. Some have even been seen drifting fully submerged and rising for air without fully waking up. It's like having a natural snorkel and waterbed combined!

SCENT-SIGNAL SPECIALISTS

Male capybaras have a scent gland on their nose called a *morillo,* which grows larger when they're in charge of a group. They rub it on plants, branches, and the ground to leave messages like a *"capy-*

bara was here" note for others to sniff. They also have **scent glands near their tails**, which they use to mark territory or show dominance.

A PANEL OF PALS

You probably know that animals like cows live in herds and fish swim in schools—but did you know a group of capybaras can be called a **panel**? So next time you see a bunch of them together, you can say, "*Look at that chill panel of capybaras!*"

FAST ON LAND, SMOOTH IN WATER

Even though they look slow and sleepy, capybaras can run surprisingly fast, up to **14 mph (about 22 km/h)**! That's faster than most humans can sprint. *And when they swim?* While scientists haven't clocked them officially, capybaras likely swim at around **3-5 mph (5-8 km/h)**—pretty fast for such a big rodent! They're so quiet they can glide unnoticed, especially when hiding from predators.

CHOMP, CHOMP, GROW!

A capybara's teeth grow about 1/8 of an inch every week! That's as much as 6 inches every year if they didn't wear them down. That's why they spend so much time chewing on tough grass and bark—to keep their ever-growing teeth at just the right length!

THE CHATTERBOXES OF THE WETLANDS

Capybaras communicate using a whole **library of sounds**—whistles, squeaks, clicks, purrs, barks, and grumbles. Each one means something different. And some scientists believe they even have unique "family calls" that help them stick together.

Wait for meeee!

YOU'RE NOW A CERTIFIED CAPY CAPTAIN!

Congratulations! You've just completed your journey through the fantastic world of capybaras. You've learned what makes these gentle giants special, from their webbed toes to their waterproof fur, peaceful personalities, and their underwater naps.

Now that you're a true capybara expert, you can proudly call yourself a **Certified Capy Captain**! The next time you visit a zoo or watch a nature show, you'll spot all the cool capybara features others might miss—and maybe even share a few fun facts of your own.

Don't forget to tell your friends and family what you've learned! Capybaras might be the world's largest rodents, but they are also some of the friendliest animals in the wild. *Who knows?* You might inspire someone else to fall in love with them, too.

And if you ever get to see a capybara in real life, remember just how remarkable they are—peaceful, playful, and perfectly at home in water and grass.

Thanks for joining us on this muddy, grassy, splashy adventure. We hope you had as much fun learning about capybaras as we did sharing their story with you.

And one last reminder: just like the capybara, being kind, calm, and friendly helps make the world a better place for everyone.

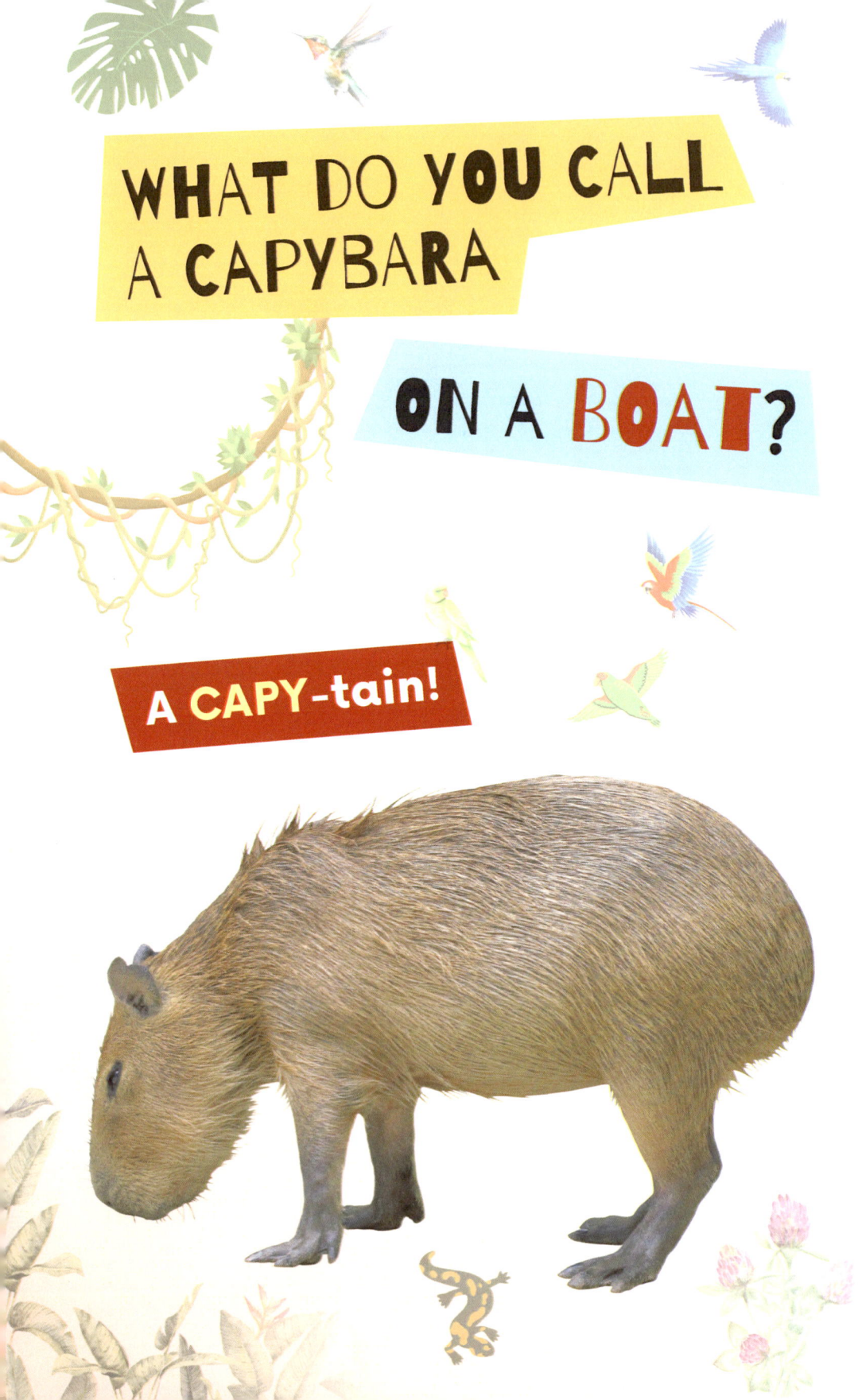

THANK YOU!

Thank you for reading this book and for allowing us to share our love for capybaras with you!

If you've enjoyed this book, please let us know by leaving a rating and a brief review wherever you made your purchase! This helps us spread the word to other readers!

Thank you for your time, and have an awesome day!

For more information, please visit:

www.animalreads.com

© Copyright 2025—All rights reserved Admore Publishing

ISBN: 978-3-96772-197-3

ISBN: 978-3-96772-198-0

ISBN: 978-3-96772-199-7

Animal Reads at www.animalreads.com

The content contained within this book may not be reproduced, duplicated or transmitted without direct written permission from the author or the publisher.

Under no circumstances will any blame or legal responsibility be held against the publisher, or author, for any damages, reparation, or monetary loss due to the information contained within this book. Either directly or indirectly.

Published by Admore Publishing: Gotenstraße, Berlin, Germany

www.admorepublishing.com

www.ingramcontent.com/pod-product-compliance
Lightning Source LLC
LaVergne TN
LVRC081131100526
838202LV00074B/2847